Collision in
The Sinking of *HMS Duchess*

Richard M. Jones

ISBN: 978-0-244-11234-9

Lodge Books
25 South Back Lane
Bridlington
www.lodgebooks.co.uk

LODGE
BOOKS

Previous page: Duchess crest at Invincible pub, Portsmouth - 4 November 2010.

This book is dedicated to the crew of *HMS Duchess.*

Duci non trahi.

Also by Richard M. Jones

The Great Gale of 1871

Lockington – Crash at the Crossing

The Burton Agnes Disaster

End of the Line – The Moorgate Disaster

Capsized in the Solent – The SRN6-012 Hovercraft Disaster

Royal Victoria Rooms – The Rise and Fall of a Bridlington Landmark

The Diary of a Royal Marine – The Life and Times of George Cutcher

Boleyn Gold (Fiction)

Introduction

It must have been over two decades ago now that an old man in the tiny Yorkshire village where I lived sat down with me as he always did and spoke about his time in the navy. The name of this former sailor was William "Bill" Doubleday and he had not only served in the Second World War but he had taken part in the 1947 Royal Tour on board *HMS Vanguard*. Serving his entire career during the war and beyond, there wasn't a place of interest that he hadn't seen or been to. As with every "matelot" he had a few stories to tell and any wartime situation brings out the most interesting and fascinating episodes, guaranteed to capture an audience at dinner tables. Bill had taken part in various major campaigns during the war years, including serving on board the battleship *HMS Barham* which was famously sunk in 1941 with heavy loss of life. Thankfully he wasn't on board, but he did have a lot of tales to tell of his time with the ship. One of those tales was of the ship that was sunk in a collision with *Barham* soon after the outbreak of conflict.

HMS Duchess wasn't a huge ship, certainly not a famous ship and in this day and age she is heard of by very few people. But when Bill told me about what happened and how quickly this took place it shocked me that I had never heard of it, and why would I… it wasn't exactly something that you would make a film about or had a huge death toll (in the grand scheme of things during the war that is). I wanted to know more about this forgotten ship and started gathering as much information as I could find. Incredibly there was very little written on the disaster or the ship itself and it has taken me around fourteen years to find what I have managed to accumulate.

Thanks to social media, the last few years have connected me with several people who had relatives who had served on the

Duchess and were able to provide photographs to give faces to these names that appear on war memorials around the country as well as the time she had spent at sea leading up to her demise.

My main passion is writing about history and focusing on forgotten disasters, in many cases this includes putting up a plaque to remember the victims and commemorate the event. For the first time, for me, I have found that there is already a memorial to this ship in a small church in Suffolk as well as the name of the ship on the war memorial at Chatham, her crew named on the panels along with tens of thousands of others who died at sea during the wars. This just leaves me to tell the story of this forgotten shipwreck and highlight the events that surround the last voyage of a Royal Navy destroyer and her crew.

In a time when hundreds of people dying at sea barely even made it into the newspapers, this book will act as a tribute to those who sailed far from home and never came back. After the loss of the *Duchess*, Britain still had almost six more years of war to get through. These were testing times for those both serving abroad and holding the fort back home. We can only imagine how it was to live in those times: houses being bombed in the cities, children evacuated and the agonising wait for that letter to say that your loved one was missing in action. By the end of the war the victory was bittersweet as very few families were left unscathed, millions were dead, thousands missing, even more were left with physical injuries and mental trauma that would live with them for the rest of their lives.

The war at sea has always been a dramatic playing field; looking back at the First World War which saw the introduction of the menace that was the U-boat and the sea mine, and terrifying stories accompanying the sinking of large vessels such as the liners *Lusitania* and *Britannic* which were considered the safest and most solid ships afloat. The response was the mine hunter, depth charges and the introduction of the Q-ships which would begin the fight-back against the submarines. World War II would be no different; in the first few months of the war a dramatic loss of shipping would lead to convoys being set up straight away and ships being redesigned to withstand something heavier than that which they had suffered during the previous twenty years. Ships would sink on a daily basis, with nothing more than a simple report buried in the newspapers giving the only indication of the loss of a proud vessel and an entire crew. There were many ships lost during the Second World War that would be forgotten about.

This is the story of one of those ships.

Duchess

1. Life and Times of a Destroyer

The name *Duchess* is not one that is new to the Royal Navy, in fact the ship that stood on the slipway at Palmers Shipbuilding and Iron Company Ltd, Hebburn-on-Tyne in the Jarrow district of Sunderland was the fourth to bear this name. Originally introduced in 1652 when a captured French ship *Duchesse* was renamed, it was then given to a 90-gun, "second rate" warship in 1679, finally being used as the name of a paddle minesweeper for a short period of time when the *Duchess of Fife* was temporarily renamed after being requisitioned by the Admiralty in the First World War. After just three years she regained her original name.

Each warship that is launched already comes with a history; every time that ship of a certain name is launched it carries with it the battle honours of all the previous ships to bear that name. In the case of the *Duchess* she carried four:

Portland	1653
Gabbard	1653
Scheveningen	1653
Barlfleur	1692

As this new Daring class destroyer was being built, she was not the first one of this class. In fact, in this case she would be the last of the nine ships to be launched and the last that this particular yard would launch of this batch. Of her eight sister ships – *Dainty, Daring, Decoy, Defender, Delight, Diamond, Diana* and *Duncan* – it was *Diana* that was laid down at the same time as *Duchess* whereas the rest were built at other shipyards around the UK.

These new destroyers had a standard displacement of 1,360 tons, had a complement of around 138 crew, although she could carry two dozen more at a squeeze, could go at a maximum speed of 35.5 knots and had a main role of normal fleet duties and convoy protection. Their armament consisted of four 4.7in guns (4x1), two 2-pounder anti-aircraft guns, eight torpedo tubes and depth charge throwers for submarine hunting.

On 16th June 1932 the *Diana* was launched, followed just over a month later, on 19th July, by the *Duchess* making her way down the slipway and into the water for the first time. The build carried on with all fixtures and fittings being added while alongside until early the following year, finally being completed on 27th January 1933 at a cost of £229,367, excluding the Admiralty-supplied equipment such as the weapons and communications equipment. She would be given the pennant number H64 which would be painted in black on the side of her hull for identification, in common with most warships. Every ship has a pennant number but not all of them display it, sometimes going as far as to paint it over completely to deny the enemy the ability to identify the ship.

Her motto would be *Duci non trahi* (To be led but not dragged) with a ship's crest unique to that name, in this case a globe with a golden crown above it on a blue background. Every ship has a motto and a crest as well as the traditional quirks that come with the ship such as a nickname or a special flag that is usually flown during replenishment operations.

*

From the moment the new destroyer left her builder's yard her ship's company were trained to a high standard; a fresh new ship straight out of the builder's always has a mountain of teething problems which need addressing. The quirks of an individual ship will soon be known and loved by their crews and *Duchess* will have been no exception. The crew will have been put through intense training with exercises in damage control, wartime situations and current affairs, much the same as the navy does today. Throwing the ship around to breaking point would be the best way to test the limits of the ship and her crew and to repair or replace anything that could go wrong. If for some reason there was a design flaw that didn't work well under exercise conditions then now was the chance to rip it out and replace it ready for when it would be used for real. The engines would be put to the test, her speed run to her highest limit, turning at high speed in avoidance procedures and emergency stopping. The list of trials a new ship has to go through is endless but during a major conflict there was never a busier or a more important time to make sure that the tests were conducted to make sure the ship was battle ready and fit for purpose.

The navy's plan for these nine new ships was to create a destroyer flotilla to be set up following various meetings and debates within the high ranking confines of the government. Passing all relevant tests and with the crew happy with the performance, *Duchess* left the Tyne on 25th January 1933 and proceeded south for her forthcoming acceptance trials. Back at sea, more tests and exercises pushed the ship to her limit once again and inspectors gave those all important ticks in the boxes for the ship to be ready for tasking.

On 16th March she sailed from a visit to Portland and headed back to her base port of Chatham where she arrived the following day, to be officially commissioned as a Royal Navy warship on 30th March under the command of Lt Cdr LJ Dover for service in the First Destroyer Flotilla, Mediterranean Fleet.

With all provisions loaded aboard and fuelled up ready for deployment she sailed south towards the Bay of Biscay, making the turn round the corner of south-western Spain to relieve the *Vivacious* and her crew of their duties. With usual naval patrols taking place, but with a full knowledge of the situation in Germany at the forefront of their minds, *Duchess* would fly the flag in many of the friendly Med ports, making stops in Gibraltar, Malta and Trieste among many others.

After a successful trip, *Duchess* returned back to base port to have a refit in 1934 in order to prepare the ship for moving away for an even longer period of time; the confirmation had come that decisions had been made from high up in navy command that she and several of her sister ships would form the 8th Destroyer Flotilla for service on the China Station, protecting Britain's interests in the Far East.

Sailing in the November of that same year she once again set off for the long trip via the Med, Suez and Indian Ocean to much hotter climes. This time *Duchess* would be replacing the *Verity* of her duties and come under the 15th Division. The ship's entire career would be spent changing duties, changing squadrons and taking over from ships already doing a job. This makes sure that patrols and tasking never have a gap and that continuous coverage takes place of the areas of interest.

By 22nd December 1934 *Duchess* had arrived in Singapore with *Duncan, Delight, Diamond* and *Daring*, the plan now being that she and her sisters would remain in the Far East for at least the next few years. Her presence would be seen mostly in Hong Kong, but she would make stops in Malaysia, Vietnam, Shanghai and Ceylon (now Sri Lanka) to name just a few.

Although the port visits would have been great for the morale of the ship's company, the voyages and patrols were routine and mostly uneventful. The only thing to note at this point was that the flotilla was renumbered in the April of that year to the 21st Flotilla.

*

Her missions were meeting success after success, exercises taking place both internally and externally with intelligence being gathered of the growing tensions within the area especially between Japan and China. In the September of 1937 the *Duchess,* together with *Duncan* and *Delight,* was stationed on the Whangpoo River, Shanghai and became engaged in bringing up British troop reinforcements from the mouth of the river to man the perimeter of the International Settlement.

On 28th September 1938, a new member of the ship's company joined the *Duchess* in the form of thirty-three-year-old Lieutenant

Commander Robert Charles Meadows White, who from this date forward would be the ship's new commanding officer. The son of a baronet, he came from Boulge Hall in Woodbridge, Suffolk and had had a naval career which began, like most Royal Naval officers, at Dartmouth College and the training ship *Thunderer*, passing out as a midshipman in January 1923 and being sent to his first proper ship *HMS Revenge*. Promoted to Sub Lt in December 1925 he rose to the rank of Lieutenant by 30th September 1927 and achieved the rank of Lieutenant Commander eight years to the day later. He had previously served on the sloop *Heliotrope* in the West Indies and the battleship *Rodney,* but from 1930 onwards he was mostly employed within the destroyers.

In 1932 he became Executive Officer (Second in command, also known as XO) of *HMS Antelope* in the Mediterranean and commanded the *Sabre* from 1935 in both Portsmouth and also in Thanet (China) where he was transferred to command the *Duchess* in September 1938. A man of obvious intelligence, during the previous year he had attended the Staff College and graduated PSC (Passed Staff College – he had undertaken the Staff Officer course).

The XO of *Duchess* was Lieutenant George Wingate Murray, the only son of the late Mr and Mrs John Congreve Murray. He had entered the RN College Dartmouth in January 1927 and went to sea as a cadet in September 1930 aboard *HMS Royal Sovereign* in the Mediterranean, being promoted to midshipman on 1st May. From October 1931 he served on the *Suffolk* in China and the battleship *Warspite* from June 1933. In March the following year he was promoted to Sub Lieutenant and after various courses he joined the largest and most famous ship in the Royal Navy, *HMS Hood* and picked up his next rank on 1st December 1935.

From the October of 1936 he served on board the destroyer *Blanche* and would join the *Duchess* in the China Station two years later after a course in signals. This was a good year for him as it was at this time he got married to Eleanor Dulcie. (It is ironic here that both his ships, *Blanche* and *Duchess,* would be lost before the end of 1939.)

Sub Lieutenant James Michael Leslie Scholfield joined the navy in January 1935 as a special entry cadet in *HMS Frobisher* and a year later passed out as a Midshipman when he was drafted to the *Hood*. From August 1936 he served on board the cruisers *Danae* (in China) and *Cornwall* (Home Fleet). He was promoted to Sub Lieutenant on 1st March 1938 and after taking the relevant courses needed he was appointed to the *Duchess* in February 1939. (He signs his name as Navigating Officer on the front of the log and gives his rank as Lieutenant.)

Lieutenant (E) Osmond Peter Tilden, the engineering officer of *Duchess*, joined the navy as a special entry cadet in *HMS Erebus* in January 1927, a year later being appointed as Midshipman (E) for the four-year course at the Royal Navy Engineering College, Keyham, during which he was promoted to Sub Lieutenant (E) from 1st June 1930. Promoted to Lieutenant (E) in 1932 he went on to serve on the cruisers *Champion* and *Exeter* in home waters, the *Dauntless* in the Mediterranean and the battleship *Royal Sovereign* in the Home Fleet. From April 1937 he was on the staff of the Mechanical Training Establishment at Chatham, a draft which he held for two years.

*

The time spent on board this ship was met with various events over the coming years. She suffered slight damage in the May of 1938 while lying at her moorings in Hong Kong when a Japanese steamer collided with her.

That same month, Japan had been interfering with foreign shipping at an alarming rate, especially those who were bound for China and, needless to say, under international law this was not permitted. Tensions arose further when a Japanese cruiser fired two shots across the bow of the P&O liner *Ranpura* which was forced to stop four miles from Hong Kong. A Japanese boarding party of four officers and a party of marines were sent on board the liner to examine her papers and ship's log, however the captain refused to comply and radioed Hong Kong for assistance. The *Duchess* was immediately sent out to intercept but thankfully the boarders quickly departed and the *Ranpura* was allowed to continue on her journey and the incident became no more than a passing annoyance instead of an international incident. Two other foreign ships were boarded and protests were lodged by all three countries at Tokyo's Foreign Office but it seemed that nothing much could be done – they seemed to just do as they pleased and disregarded these laws, which was getting to be a worry because the same thing was happening in Europe; the last thing the world needed was two sides of the globe having countries escalating situations and raising tensions.

These tensions had already reached a new high after a Japanese landing force took over the Fujian Province on 13th May 1938, threatening the security of the city of Foochow. Sure enough the *Duchess* and *Daring* were caught up in the hostilities and within days the area came under aerial attack. Between 31st May and 1st June several Chinese gunboats were sunk, with the entire port being blockaded following the placement of booms across the river. With so much happening in this area of the world it would be a miracle if any of these ships came away unscathed.

It was obvious to those back in the UK that things were not looking good for the regions of the Far East and the Royal Navy had to be on high alert for things escalating further. In December 1938, she paid a visit to Sharp Peak at Foochow and the few days that the ship then spent there were meticulously documented in a report by her captain.

HMS Duchess – Report of Proceeding
Sharp Peak 16-20 December 1938
Report by RCM White, CO, *HMS Duchess*
I have the honour to forward a report of proceedings of *HM Ship Duchess* under my command for the period of duty as Senior Naval Officer at Sharp Peak and during my visit to Foochow.

The report states that the ship arrived at Sharp Peak at 0800 on 16th December and left at 1715 on 20th December bound for Swatow (aka Shantou). It seemed that there was very little for the ship's company to do for entertainment other than "picknicking and sailing" along with some walking parties taking in the views on the island. *Duchess* was anchored and it was evident that it was a case of first come first served with the berthing arrangements; depending on when you arrived would determine which anchorage you were allocated.

Ten of the ship's ratings were sent ashore to visit the consulate and were not only accommodated there but also given use of the Customs Club, where they "were looked after in the most hospitable manner" with dinner parties also hosted here. On 17th December there were the official calls to the Provincial Chairman, General and Admiral followed by the usual cocktail party that evening, again held at the Consulate.

With launch boats provided to take the ship's company over the water to shore, the Captain was taken to some of the parts of the nearby surrounding areas in order to show him the work being done in the community and how dependent it was on the few foreigners that were doing it. All the schools and hospitals he saw were run by missionaries and White seemed pleased to be going around seeing all this as usually he only ever met dignitaries and the usual VIPs, but this experience had him talking to members of the public and finding out just what was really going on and what their thoughts and personal experiences were.

Among the things White discussed with the consulate were the evacuation plans of the locals and expatriates should an emergency arise. Tensions were already rising in the area between China and Japan and a lot of people were naturally on their guard. Despite this the locals were not as nervous as outsiders had liked to believe. However, a list of British and other residents, for which HBM Consul (Mr RA Hall) was responsible, was discussed and submitted to HM Embassy at Shanghai.

Not limiting his visits to only the British locals, White called on the Provincial Chairman Ch'en Yi, General Ch'en Ch'I and Admiral Lee. Lee showed great interest in discussing the theoretical laying of mines in the shipping channels, the visits of warships and the depths of the channels.

Overall nobody here seemed to be specifically expecting an attack by the Japanese. In the more quiet days pre-Pearl Harbour, many of the residents may have been under the impression that the whole episode would just blow over and they would all carry on as normal.

White got to work on sending his report, describing the port as a very large trading port with as many as a dozen ships from six nationalities loading at Sharp Peak. Despite the locals being so calm about the situations that were arising, White seemed more concerned that a storm was brewing with the Japanese and that it would not just blow over and be forgotten over time. The evacuation plan would be written down and circulated to HM ships so they would know what to expect if they were present during an emergency. Lines of communication would be set up by the use of runners passing messages between the consulate and local organisations, with motor launches ferrying evacuees up the river to safety which could take as many as eighty people at a time. Refugee camps would then be able to be set up at the schools and hospitals. Following the end of the compilation of the report, he attached a list of the names of everybody who would need to be evacuated and where they would be located. As he finished the final parts of his report and sailed from Foochow, he would have wondered what the future held for the port and if it would be his ship that would have to step up to help when – not if – the expected emergencies arose.

It would only be a matter of time before friendly talks broke down, tensions would escalate and physical action would commence. When that time would come was anybody's guess.

Duchess

Duchess (Luis Photos Gibraltar)

Duchess (Maritime Picture Library)

Duchess in China

14

Duchess cutter boarding party on a Japanese vessel

Duchess crew under canvas

Duchess crew under canvas while ship is being refitted.
Stonecutters Island, Hong Kong

2. The Journey Home

1939 was a year of major change in Europe. German leader Adolf Hitler had been flexing the muscles of his National Socialist German Workers Party (more commonly known as the Nazi Party) across the countries bordering Germany. An Austrian by birth, Hitler first annexed Austria, much to the disapproval of the world. With no real action taken against him he did the same to Czechoslovakia and once again the world stood by and watched. With the threat of further invasions being imminent, Britain stood up and announced that if Hitler went any further and made the moves to invade Poland then war would be declared.

Sure enough on 1st September 1939 German troops marched into Poland and, as promised, two days later war was declared against Germany. In a move that would rock the world, this would be the second major conflict in twenty-one years between the two sides, everybody having been so confident that the 1914-1918 conflict would be "the war to end all wars," so much so that it was simply known as The Great War.

At the time of the outbreak the *Duchess* was still on China Station, with Admiral Sir Percy Noble in overall command. Despite problems in southern Asia the seven units of the Flotilla were ordered by the Admiralty to return to the UK. *Duchess* had sailed on 2nd September from Singapore after being alongside the ex *RFA Ruthenia,* where she had topped up on fuel and provisions before she headed out to sea on her regular patrols. Following the news of the declaration of war, her entry into the log on 3rd September simply said, "1750 Commenced hostilities against Germany," and it was signed by the ship's twenty-two-year-old Navigating Officer, James Scholfield.

Two days later she arrived at the port of Trincomalee in Ceylon (today known as Sri Lanka) and secured alongside another

RFA. (Her log states *Boardale* and then changes to what looks like *Orcades*, but *Orcades* didn't exist as an RFA and *Boardale* was not on record as being there.) *Duchess* stayed there until 1000 on 7th September when she took just twenty-one hours to get to Colombo and secured alongside *HMS Delight*. She wasn't there long when at 1100 the same day *Duchess*, *Delight* and *Decoy* left port and sailed away together.

As the journey home progressed, the ships would alter the clocks as they slowly made their way over the time zones, every few days getting that little bit closer to UK time. Greenwich Mean Time is also known as Zulu Time in the military, with the letters corresponding with whichever time zone you head towards. If you were to head east from the UK you would head into Alpha Time, Bravo Time and so on. If you were to head west across the Atlantic then you would go in the opposite direction, changing to Yankee Time, X-Ray Time and back. (British Summer time would be known as Alpha time as it is Zulu +1). When a ship has been away for such a long period of time, this is actually an exciting part of returning home, knowing that you are that bit closer to home that you are almost in the same time zone.

The captain of the *Duchess*. Lt Cdr Robert White during a crossing the line ceremony, 1938.

Crossing the line ceremony

On 14th September 1939 the task group called in to the Yemeni port of Aden, securing to a buoy at 0825 with the captain making a call on *Delight* during the day. Two other warships were there already: *HMS Liverpool* and *HMS Seal*, the latter having been there since the outbreak of war.

The following day, at 0900 on 15th September the *Duchess* weighed anchor and left harbour in company with *Liverpool*, *Delight* and *Defender* heading north up the Red Sea. During the day it became obvious that one of the members of her ship's company was seriously ill with heat stroke. In the early afternoon the *Delight* and *Duchess* closed each other (this means both ships coming towards each other until they are both at a safe distance away to conduct a task) and at 1425 the Medical Officer on board *Delight* was transferred over to see Stoker 1st Class William Walker. Things must have been serious for a transfer to have taken place so soon after leaving the confines of the harbour. As in all countries in the Middle East the temperature can reach so high that it is not advisable to work in those conditions. (Author's note – I personally have been out in 130 degree Fahrenheit heat before in these areas and it is not only exhausting but you lose so much water in dehydration you need a constant supply of fluids.)

It soon became apparent that there was nothing the doctor could do as Walker had suffered heart failure and died that afternoon, he was aged just thirty-six. At 1740 the Medical Officer was transferred back onto *Delight* and the ships continued their passage while the rest of the crew mourned the loss of their shipmate. The death was listed as being, "Cardiac failure after heat prostration."

Heat prostration is also known as heatstroke or hyperthermia (not to be confused with hypothermia caused by extreme cold). It is the overheating of the body due to extreme weather conditions. Unrelieved hyperthermia can lead to collapse and death, particularly in the elderly. Prevention via air conditioning, ventilation, and drinking extra amounts of water is the key for any vulnerable persons.

On the morning of 16th September, at 0900 the *Duchess* stopped in the middle of the Red Sea between Saudi Arabia and Eritrea. A short service took place and the body of William Walker was buried at sea. Just fifteen minutes later the ship was underway once more. The items that were used by Walker were destroyed as being unfit for use – namely two blankets, one mattress and one mattress cover.

*

On the early morning of Monday 18th September 1939, the ship slowed down at the very top of the Red Sea, for now she had reached the entrance to the Suez Canal and at 0600 proceeded to anchor close by to await further instructions. Opened in 1869, this waterway was a godsend to ships that had previously gone all the way around the southern tip of Africa if they wanted to go to/from the Mediterranean into the Indian Ocean and the Red Sea. Now in just one day ships could make the journey through the canal which cut a channel right through Egypt and provided a huge income for the country from the amount of shipping that was to use it.

At 0815 a pilot was embarked with the ship weighing anchor fifteen minutes later and proceeded to enter the canal and slowly transit the narrow channel at a speed of eight knots. With an exchange of pilots halfway, the *Duchess* arrived at Port Said in the Mediterranean at 1650. She would stay at anchor overnight and proceed into the northern Egyptian port of Alexandria alongside the *Delight* later that day, taking oil from the tanker *Brambleleaf*. That evening the ship was secured to a buoy with *Delight* and the ship's company would spend the next few days carrying out general maintenance on the ship including painting.

On Sunday 24th September 1939, the usual Sunday church service took place at 0900 which was followed by a set of divisions at 0950, because today they had a very special visitor – Vice Admiral John C. Tovey C.B. D.S.O.

Tovey had been given the task of commanding the destroyers

in the Mediterranean and keeping a sharp eye on events surrounding the Spanish Civil War which had been ongoing for the last few years. Despite the fact that the Civil War had ended the previous April it was still a highly volatile area, especially now Europe was at war. (Tovey would later become famous for his role in the chasing and sinking of the German battleship *Bismarck* in 1941.)

On 26th September it was time for *Duchess* to go back to sea; this time she would stay in the area and run exercises with *Delight* initially and then, after a brief return to port, she would then meet up and work with the bigger warships such as *Barham, Malaya, Warspite, Glorious* and *Gallant.* Air attacks would be exercised on the afternoon of the 28th as aircraft from the aircraft carrier *Glorious* "attacked" the *Duchess* and provided some good training for the gun crews of *Duchess* as well as for the aircrews of the *Glorious* based aircraft.

By the morning of the 29th *Duchess* and *Defender* were detached from the exercises and proceeded back to Port Said by that evening. It was here that the ship boarded a new Midshipman the following afternoon, CL Kretschmer RNR, a nineteen-year-old officer who would now call *Duchess* his home and learn on the job the skills needed to become a sub lieutenant. Just hours later he would get his first taste of life on board this ship as late into the night the *Duchess* slipped and proceeded to sea at 2250. This time the ship had a different type of mission and one that was sure to need all the air attack training possible; the ship was now assigned to convoy duty.

*

By the early morning of Sunday 1st October 1939, a convoy of twenty-one ships had formed up overnight, which included the warships *Grimsby, Duchess* and *Defender.* Codenamed "Blue 003" it was their mission to safely proceed across the Mediterranean Sea with twenty-two merchant ships, a further two joining later.

Although the voyage was less than two weeks from start to finish, the fear of air and U-boat attacks was on everybody's mind and a sharp lookout would have been kept on all ships and in every direction. The mission was to get these twenty-four ships between Port Said and Gibraltar without incident, a few ships leaving slightly earlier to continue their own journey.

In a convoy system it was customary for the warships to surround the merchant ships in order to offer protection from all sides, in this case each one would take a sector and the rest of the civilian ships would sail close by in a group. Although these ships would most likely have arms on board to defend themselves should the worst happen, having a warship escort was far more effective. Destroyers alone carried a stack of depth charges all set and ready to deploy if the need arose. *Duchess* could drop them over the side or fire them into the air to get some distance. Everybody hoped they would not need to be used, but all defences were prepared just in case.

In the meantime, they would spend the next few days zigzagging, while other ships joined them including the warship *Fowey*. Incredibly there was very little to report and the time had come for two warships to depart the convoy and be relieved by *Grenade* and *Griffin,* which then took over the duties of *Duchess* and *Defender*. At 0600 on 5th October the SS *British Sergeant* was also detached with the two warships to head to Malta together. Being close to the island already, it was that afternoon that all of them were tied up alongside safe and sound in Grand Harbour.

As for the convoy, all the ships arrived at their destinations; most of them entered Gibraltar on 11th October, one headed to Algiers and another was left behind and took care of themselves. (In a wartime situation a convoy of that size could not wait for slow ships with problems to catch up, especially if the cargo being carried was high value; there was just too much risk to the other ships and slowing down twenty-plus ships for one straggler was not worth it. For example, in 1942 the liner *Queen Mary* was carrying thousands of troops across the Atlantic when she accidentally

23

rammed the cruiser *HMS Curacoa*, ripping her in half and leaving hundreds dead. *Queen Mary* continued to her destination at full speed due to the risk of losing thousands of lives should the ship come under attack by U-boats which had been ordered to sink the liner at the earliest opportunity. Thankfully the survivors of the cruiser were rescued by the smaller ships in the convoy.)

Diamond, Duchess and *Delight* alongside Malta.

Duchess sailed out of Grand Harbour on the morning of 12th October 1939 and that afternoon met up with the destroyers *Grafton* and *Gallant* to form a screen, their job being to challenge merchant ships in the area and if needed board them. Together they headed west and arrived at Gibraltar's northern entrance two days later to embark fuel and stores. She would spend the next few days here and on 15th October two ratings – Petty Officer Anderson and able rating George Passmore – were discharged sick on shore to the Royal Naval Hospital up by Europa Point.

Gibraltar had been a port of call for British navy vessels ever since the capture of the town by Admiral Rooke in 1704. Since then it had been a place that sailors loved to go and it is as much loved now as it was then; very British and a taste of home but with sunshine. With a main street running through the town centre at the bottom of a large mountain, Gibraltar has always affectionately been known simply as "The Rock", and for as long as anybody could remember sailors would take part in the Rock Run, a race to see who would be first to run up the roads right to the very top and back down again in the fastest time. Not only are there sights to see from the top, such as the airport (where the main road into Spain crosses over the runway) and the tunnels from the siege of 1779, but the biggest attraction is that this is the only place in Europe where wild apes are free to roam. Most of the time they are quite peaceful but they have been known to be aggressive if something makes them feel threatened, such as a tourist getting too close to their young. At the time of the Second World War, tunnels were being fitted out for use by the military and the height of the rock became a huge advantage in controlling shipping coming in and out of the Mediterranean. The Rock was such an important territory that it is said that those who control Gibraltar control the Mediterranean.

It was the evening of 17th October that *Duchess* was back at sea questioning merchant ships and continued heading eastbound back to Malta. A three-day journey that would see another new joiner arrive on the 20th in the form of Lieutenant Pritchard RNVR who had joined from *HMS Nubian*. He will have most likely taken over from the lieutenant who left the ship the following day on passage to the UK. Another one leaving the ship just an hour before sailing was an unknown rating who was discharged to St Angelo for forty-two days detention. There is no record of who he was or why he was sent to a military detention, nor is there any record of him returning to ship. Had his detention time saved his life or did he rejoin the ship later on just in time to make the journey back to the UK? Either way, the ship left harbour at 1700 that afternoon and began a new mission.

*

The *Duchess* was now tasked to relieve the *Diana* and take over her duties of the Kithera Patrol. After a handover the latter ship was to head back to Alexandria while *Duchess* would query ships in the area and conduct boardings where they felt it was necessary. The sea must have been getting a bit rough as their log states that on 26th October the crew were employed securing the upper deck gear, but a 3-inch drill cartridge and a drill fuse were both lost overboard in the process. Then a rating on board was injured, probably due to the ship rolling around; again we don't know the extent of his injuries but it was enough for the ship to alter course to head back to Malta. It would be another twenty-four hours or so of travelling but she arrived back to the island and was able to have the injured crewman landed. If that wasn't bad enough, a further two ratings went along with him to the Royal Naval Hospital (known as RNH Bighi) with medical issues.

With several people in both Malta and Gibraltar hospitals there was now a significant gap in the ship's manpower, but this issue was resolved on 28th October when two ratings from the *Duncan* were brought on board, although two days later two further ratings were sent ashore sick. Thankfully the ship was to be docked down for a short period of time, along with *Duncan*; the ship's company would be busy with maintenance jobs at least for the foreseeable future. At around midday on 31st October the ship was high and dry with the hands employed with various refit tasks.

Before too long the ship was back in the water and ready to get back to work. She sailed once again on 16th November to escort the liner *Franconia* while at the same time she was used for screening and contraband control, carrying out patrols and searching neutral ships for contraband of war. Before long she was detached with two of her sister ships, *Dainty* (Cdr. F.M. Walton, RN) and *Delight* (Cdr. M. Fogg-Elliot, RN) as part of the escort for the battleship *HMS Barham* on her passage from the Mediterranean to home waters.

The *Barham* (Capt. H.T.C. Walker, RN) was a Queen Elizabeth class battleship of 33,000 tons, built at John Brown and Co, Clydebank in 1915. As a brand new ship she was stationed at Rosyth at the time of the Battle of Jutland in May 1916 and sailed straight away only to face a barrage of fire from the German fleet, narrowly escaping disaster following a hit near B turret. That particular battle was a huge loss to both sides with the Royal Navy losing several major warships with horrific death tolls.

HMS Barham

That was twenty-three years ago and now *Barham* had been in the Mediterranean for eighteen months and was alongside Alexandria (Egypt) at the outbreak of war. She had been in no great hurry to return to the UK but with no real threat in the area it was decided that her presence around the home waters would be better.

Meanwhile the *Duchess* had another member of the ship's company join – Stoker Thomas Gilham had rejoined *Duchess* at Alexandria from *HMS Nile* on 27th November. (This was a shore base at Alexandria also known as Ras el Tin Point.) *Duchess* was soon back at sea while the rest of the task force prepared for the two-week trip back to the UK. It was now time for *Barham* to sail and head for home at last; she set sail back to Scotland, slipping out of the harbour at 0700 on Friday 1st December escorted by *Defender* and *Dainty*.

Duncan sailed from Malta at 0831 on 2nd December and by 1750 that evening sighted the *Duchess*. On Sunday 3rd, after *Barham* had been at sea for two days and Malta was now far behind her, she was joined by *Duncan* and *Duchess* which were to relieve the *Defender* and *Dainty* to accompany her on the journey home.

Along the way the ships would need to call back in to Gibraltar, although this would only be a short visit. For this task group they would only be staying long enough for them to refuel and take on stores, fresh water and ammunition, arriving late in the afternoon of 5th December. Doing the same as every other short port visit, the task group was ready to go and they sailed for the final time on Wednesday 6th December for the last but longest leg of the journey home, out into the cold stormy Atlantic and north through the Bay of Biscay towards home waters. After five years away from home, the crew of these destroyers were at last getting closer to their home country and, most importantly, their families who were waiting patiently for them to come home. Wartime or not, there was no better feeling than arriving home after a long period of absence.

**Military Hospital Gibraltar where two crew members were taken
on her last port visit.**

*

At the western side of the Scottish coastline lies the River Clyde, a stretch of water that is renowned for the ships of the navy as well as the vast merchant fleets. For decades ships were built here from the small ships of the navy to the huge transatlantic liners that graced the waves from the early part of the 20th century. Names like *Lusitania, Mauritania, Queen Elizabeth* and *Queen Mary* had all plied these waters and had become household names. The largest ship in the Royal Navy at the time, *HMS Hood*, had been built at the very same yards as had the *Barham*. Now the entire area from Glasgow up to Greenock was a hive of activity with ships coming and going every day.

It was on Saturday 9th December 1939 that three ships, the *Echo, Eclipse* and *Exmouth* all weighed anchor in the dead of night and proceeded together out into the Irish Sea and headed northwest

29

towards the tip of Northern Ireland. Their job was like the previous tasks they had been given, namely to escort a capital ship back into the Clyde safely and be on the lookout for enemy activity.

Two days later on 11th December, the *Barham* and her escort group were coming into focus and by mid afternoon all three ships had not only sighted them, they had joined up and taken station with *Eclipse* on the starboard bow of *Barham* on a course of 030 and a speed of sixteen knots. Just before midnight the ships all sighted the Inishtrahull light and knew that it would only be a matter of hours until Scotland was in sight up ahead.

Now going at around eighteen knots, the task force, now consisting of *Barham, Duncan, Duchess, Exmouth, Eclipse* and *Echo,* all headed out of international waters and further towards the UK, rounding the coast and heading towards the top of the Irish Sea and their final destination of the River Clyde.

*

While the story of any ships involved with historic events are always talked about and the names are easily recognisable, those who served on board these vessels are very rarely mentioned. With the exception of a few high ranking Admirals or VC winners, few sailors are written about. Everybody knows the names of Nelson, Collingwood, Drake and Raleigh – so much so we still have naval bases named after them. But the regular ratings and the people who ran the ships on a day-to-day basis are one among thousands. So here are the profiles of a few of those sailors on board the *Duchess* who are remembered today by their families and who have shared personal details in order for their lives to be documented and remembered.

Stoker 1st Class Thomas Gilham was born on 13th September 1919 in Hove and went to school in Margate, Kent before moving to Peckham in London. He joined the navy and was later part of the naval base at *HMS Pembroke.* Just before he joined *Duchess* out in the Far East he wrote a three-page letter to his parents telling them of his trip (see illustrations).

Thomas Gilham (left)

A letter home sent by Thomas Gilham:

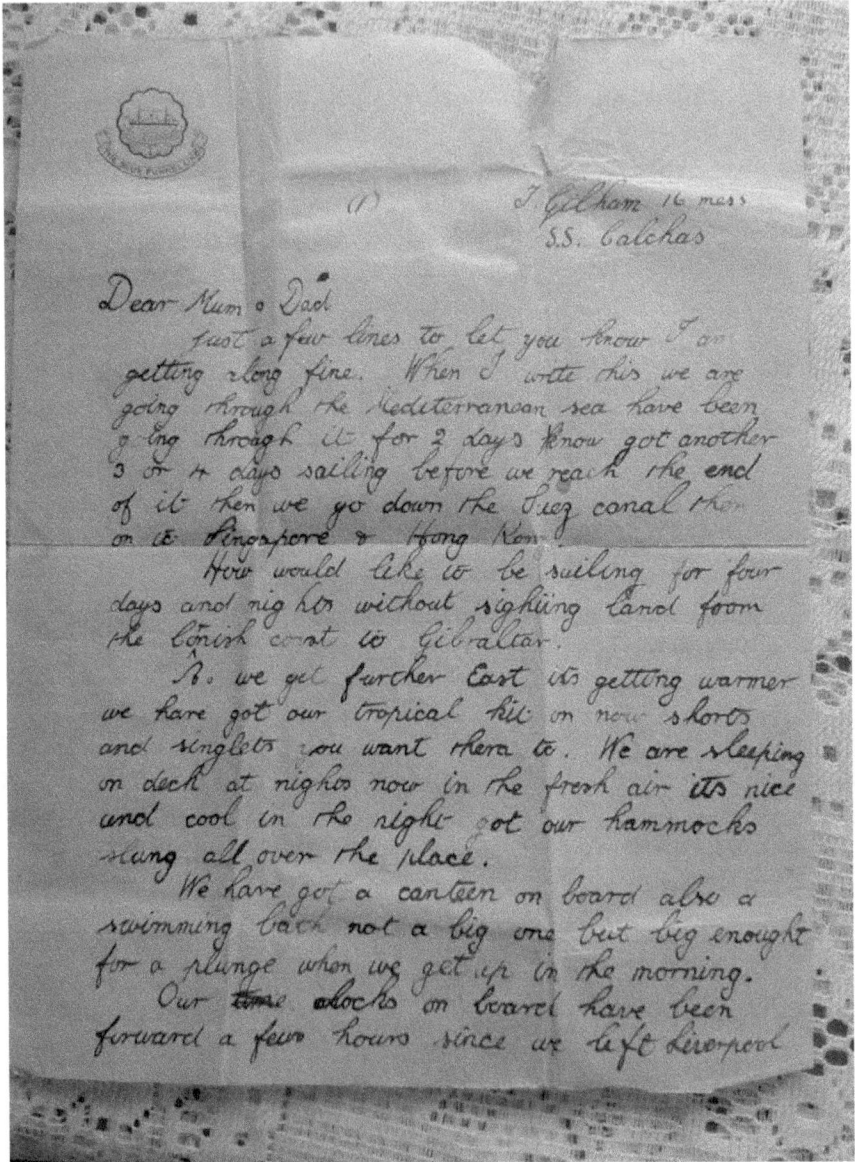

(1)   T. Gilham 16 mess
                                 S.S. Calchas

Dear Mum & Dad
        Just a few lines to let you know I am
getting along fine. When I write this we are
going through the Mediterranean sea have been
going through it for 2 days know got another
3 or 4 days sailing before we reach the end
of it then we go down the Suez canal then
on to Singapore & Hong Kong.
        How would like to be sailing for four
days and nights without sighting land from
the Cornish coast to Gibraltar.
        As we get farther East its getting warmer
we have got our tropical kit on now shorts
and singlets you want them to. We are sleeping
on deck at nights now in the fresh air its nice
and cool in the night got our hammocks
slung all over the place.
        We have got a canteen on board also a
swimming bath not a big one but big enough
for a plunge when we get up in the morning.
        Our time clocks on board have been
forward a few hours since we left Liverpool

32

(2)

All we have to do after dinner every day is
lay about in the sun or read, its lovely weather
the seas been pretty calm except for a few heavy
swells off the Irish sea. We might go ashore
at Port Said dont now for sure but if we
do it will be the first time we set foot on
dry land for about 10 days if we dont it
will be another 16 days before we reach
Penang on the China coast talk about a life
on the ocean waves.

We reach our destination Hong Kong on
September 5th. By the way I found out
the name of my boat the night before we
left so I could not let you know it is
a destroyer HMS Duchess.

Dont write yet for 2 or 3 weeks because
a letter takes about 20 days to get out
here and we will not get to Hong Kong before
about 30 more days. Sending it overland via
Siberia it gets here quickest. If it is sent by
boat we would get them in 6 weeks I'll enclose
the address. We lets know how tricks are
in London, we find out a bit by wireless
on the boat the news is typewritten and pinned
on notice board on the mess deck

33

Hows Bill getting on and yourself & family
remember me to the customers and the Mycrofts
Ken ought to be out here in Mediteranean if
he wants to get sunburnt, all our draft
have caught the sun walking about in shorts
and singlets.

You get some lovely scenery here in
the Med, the mountains with snow on the
tops on the Spanish and North african shores
I ought to have fetched my camera so I
could send a few snaps home so you could
see what its like. Well I'll have to
close now remember me to all

x x x x

Tom

P.S. The address is

Stoker Mess
C/KX93230
HMS Duchess
c/o G.P.O. London
China Station
via Siberia

34

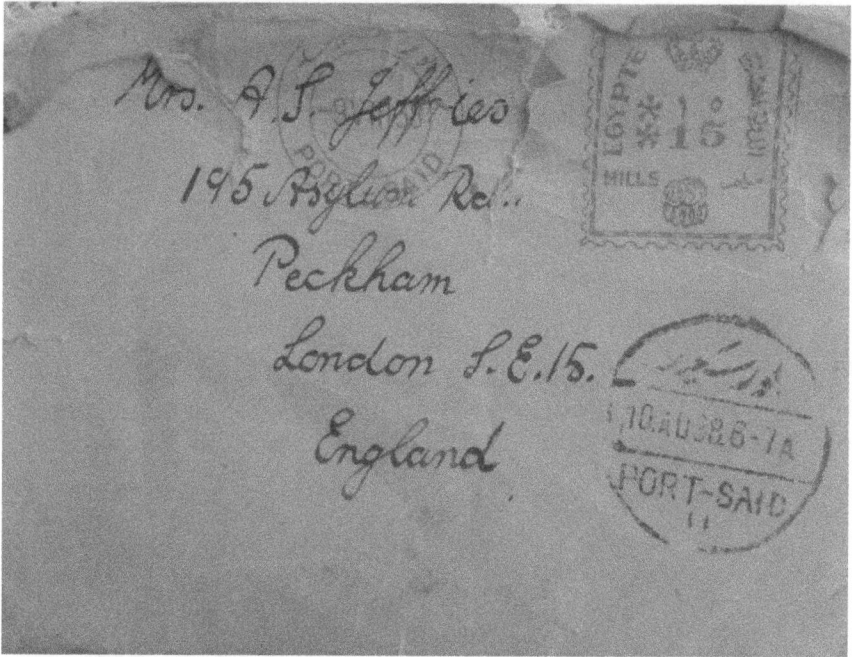

Mrs. A.J. Jeffries
195 Asylum Rd.
Peckham
London S.E.15.
England

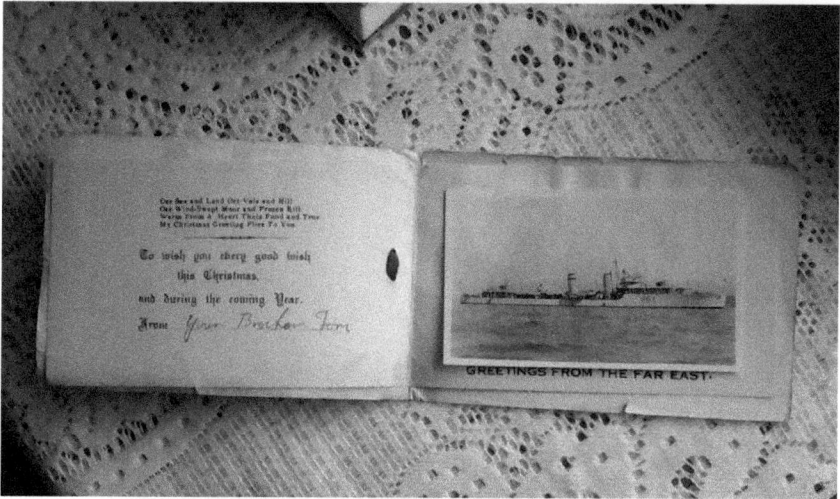

Christmas card sent to sister of Thomas "Tommy" Gilham
(owned by Peggy Harper - Tommy's niece)

Season's Greetings 8th Destroyer Flotilla

For muchee long time no have see,
Old fiend across the sea,
One litty Card me sendee you,
Talkey Melly Klismas, and New year too.

H.M.S. DUCHESS

Xmas 1938

China

Oer Sea and Land Oer Vale and Hill
Oer Wind-Swept Moor and Proses Rill
Warm From A Heart Thats Fond and True
My Christmas Greeting Flies To You

To wish you every good wish
this Christmas,
and during the coming Year.
From Your Brother Tom

GREETINGS FROM THE FAR EAST

Twenty-five-year-old **Leading Stoker Percy Small Hayward** came from a family that already had a military background. His mother, Elsie Hayward was in service to the Knox Darcy family, in the Earls Court area, when she was just sixteen and in 1911 she fell for a soldier named Small who was later killed at the very start of the First World War. She found that she was pregnant by him and with the realisation that she would be having her baby alone, she went home to her parents in Ashford where she gave birth to baby Percy. She then went off to Dartmouth and married, emigrating to Canada with her new husband which now left Percy to be raised by his grandmother, uncles and aunts. It is not known why Percy did not go with them but when he was older he joined the navy, ending up on the *Duchess* on this passage to destiny.

Able rating George Edward Taylor, aged twenty-one, was born and brought up in Salmston Road in Margate, Kent, attending Salmston Road School. Another one who signed up from an early age, he wouldn't be the only sailor in the family; his brother Edward also joined the navy.

Ordinary Seaman Kenneth Arthur Hoult was eighteen years old when he was on the *Duchess*. The eldest son of Arthur and Nellie Hoult, it was a big family with a pair of younger brothers, Alan and Ray, and his sister Irene living at the family home at 25 Dormer Avenue, Bolehall, Tamworth. Educated at Tamworth Boys Council School in Hospital Street he regularly attended services at St Editha's Parish Church in the town and after leaving school he found employment at Tamworth Colliery, but went on to join the navy in 1938 after realising that this was his ambition.

He underwent training at Chatham and was drafted to his first ship, the *Duchess*. Before the ship left the Mediterranean on her final voyage he was one of those admitted to a naval hospital with a minor illness. At this point his main worry was missing the ship sailing and being apart from his shipmates. He returned back on board much to his relief, not realising that fate was to play another hand in his life before the journey was out.

Lieutenant Osmond Peter Tilden was born at Epsom in Surrey on 8th March 1909. The son of Harry Tilden, Secretary of the Bank of England, and Ada (nee Osmond) Tilden of "Selma", he lived at 6 Ashdown Road, Epsom in Surrey and had been educated at Lancing College where he was in Olds House from January 1923 to December 1926. He gained his School Certificate in 1926 and was a Sergeant in the Officer Training Corps achieving Certificate A in 1926. In January 1927, he entered the Royal Navy as a special entry Cadet on the gunnery training monitor *HMS Erebus* and he was appointed as a Midshipman in 1928 to go on to the Royal Naval Engineering College at Keyham for a four-year course.

Tilden was promoted to Sub Lieutenant on 1st June 1930 and married at Devonport in the following year to Sophia Hilda (nee Ife) of Devonport, Devon. He had only been Sub Lieutenant for just over two years when he was promoted again, this time achieving the rank of Lieutenant on 1st October 1932, at which time he had served in home waters with the light cruiser *HMS Champion* and the heavy cruiser *Exeter*. His travels with the navy took him on board the light cruiser *Dauntless* in the Mediterranean and later with the battleship *Royal Sovereign* as part of the Home Fleet.

For two years from April 1937 he was on the staff of the Mechanical Training Establishment at Chatham and was later posted to the *Duchess* as her Engineering Officer.

*

Now in the middle of the night, the task force steamed towards the Scottish coast, as in the distance up ahead shone the light of the Mull of Kintyre. Their final destination after five years away was literally just around the corner. With lookouts on the bridge of each ship watching carefully for any sign of the enemy, it would be ironic that the greatest danger would be from themselves.

Torpedo party - George Wilkie (rear 2nd from left) and Arthur Graham (rear 3rd from right)

Thomas Gilham with lads from *HMS Pembroke*

George Forrest

Percy Small Hayward at the front door of
home, 26 West Street, Ashford, Kent

**Leading Seaman William Burt (died) far right,
with signalman Charles Merry (survived) next to him.**

George Edward Taylor

3. Collision and Confusion

The early morning of Tuesday 12th December 1939 saw the fleet of six ships heading down the north-eastern coast of Ireland in very dark conditions especially with all ships showing no lights so as not to betray their presence to the U-boats. Anti-submarine escort duty involved several destroyers spread out to form a screen with the high value unit in the middle (in this case *Barham*); this had been routinely practised in daytime and exercised in peacetime, but not in wartime in pitch black.

One of the main problems of transiting across the sea in these conditions was that the crew had to rely on estimating distance and keeping station properly by the use of binoculars and good lookouts, these being the days before the use of radar which was still a new invention at this point and certainly rarely used on board warships. What made it more difficult was that part of the anti-submarine procedure was to zigzag as a group to make it more difficult for the submarines to hit you with torpedoes. This had worked fine in the convoy system that they had previously employed so there was no reason why it should be any different now.

As they approached the North Channel some nine miles from the Mull of Kintyre, Scotland, the task force altered course to head towards the entrance to the River Clyde. The escorting destroyers had to make their move first with the *Barham* following suit.

At 0425 *Barham* altered course 45 degrees to starboard and as she steadied on her new course the *Duchess* seemed to have underestimated the distance and cut across the bows of the battleship. With no room to correct the mistake both ships now found themselves in a situation that was unavoidable. With seconds to react, those who were able to would have braced for impact, but nothing could stop the collision. At 0427 the bows of the huge ship slammed into the *Duchess* abreast the fo'c'sle, cutting deep into the hull. The sound of tearing metal as the battleship's full weight and speed pushed deep into the destroyer reverberated throughout both ships. The two ships were separated and the smaller *Duchess* immediately started taking on water, capsizing straight away and flinging the lucky few crew members into the sea. With the realisation of the horrors that had just come upon them, the *Barham* had to react immediately and attempt to limit what was already a major disaster. Within seconds it was realised that *Duchess* was doomed, it was just a matter of retrieving as many of those alive as they could. For those now finding themselves swimming for their lives it became apparent that their fight for survival had only just begun. With oil already in the water with debris and the threat of fire, they were now surrounded by huge warships that could easily run them over in the dark. Or worse, they could be carried out to sea without anybody even noticing.

*

The confusion surrounding what happened next can only be told by those who were there. Surrounding the area of the collision were the remaining escort ships as well as the *Barham* and it is from these ships' logs that we can gain an idea of just what was going on and at what exact time each ship had the same experiences.

Duncan reported at 0430 that they were to close the *Barham*, six minutes later the ship was brought to action stations as searchlights and chaos left the ship in no doubt that this was most likely an enemy attack. *Echo* reported at 0437 that the *Barham* had signalled her to join her, with *Duncan* realising very quickly that the scene they were looking at was that of an overturned vessel which they quickly illuminated with their own searchlights. At 0450 both *Echo* and *Duncan* stopped in the water and launched their whalers (boats) and began a hasty search for survivors. Within minutes of the alarm being raised it was obvious that the upturned hull was the *Duchess* and that she had been struck by the *Barham*, her crew who were lucky enough to have been thrown off the upper deck struggling in the water. Ships' positions were recorded which showed the light of the Mull of Kintyre to be around nine miles away, each ship giving a different bearing due to them all now facing in different directions as the search and rescue got underway. In the freezing waters of the northern Irish Sea the life expectancy of somebody thrown overboard with possible injuries would be measured in just minutes. The quicker the survivors were picked up the more chance they had of being alive before hypothermia set in. In winter, off the coast of Scotland is probably one of the worst places to be swimming around, especially in the dark.

The Officer of the Watch on board the lead destroyer *Duncan* had seen *Barham* switch on her searchlights, illuminating what they initially thought was a U-boat that had been rammed by the battleship.

The truth soon became clear to all the ships that this was not a submarine – what they were actually seeing was the underneath of the *Duchess* and her red hull sticking up, her ASDIC dome giving the impression of a conning tower. It is easy to see how they could have been confused in such a situation especially with so many unknowns factored into the equation.

Soon after 5am explosions rocked the upturned *Duchess* as her own depth charges, which had been primed ready for use, detonated as they fell free and reached the depth at which they had been set, exploding and sending columns of water up and igniting fires all around the stricken wreck. It was these explosions that killed some of the crew still struggling in the water. Within minutes the ship had gone, sunk beneath the cold dark waters leaving nothing but a small amount of wreckage, a few survivors and an oil slick.

By now it was clear that the few crew who had survived had been taken on board the *Barham*, who had been quick in launching her boats straight after the collision and rescuing those few who were now still alive. With no more survivors to be seen the *Echo* and *Duncan* hoisted their boats back on board and continued their search of the vicinity with not much hope of finding anybody else still alive. By 0730 the *Echo's* log states that she entered the large oil patch that now decorated the surface and at 0750 *Eclipse* did the same. It soon became apparent that there was nothing more to be done.

By 0800 the search had been completed without any luck, and the ships reformed their task force and continued their journey towards the River Clyde, by now only a few hours sailing time away.

*

John Davies on board the *Barham* tells the story from his point of view: "At the time of the collision with *Duchess* I was lookout on the portside of the bridge. It was a cold night with a blizzard blowing and I did report a destroyer passing from port to starboard but because of the very bad weather no one saw *Duchess*. When we collided the big ships stopped and all searchlights were switched on. After *Duchess* had turned over the depth charges and boilers blew up at the same time some of the crew were seen to be attempting to escape through the portholes.

"One man was found on *Barham's* torpedo blisters and one hanging onto the anchor. One of *Barham's* midshipmen dived overboard and I think he pulled some out. We continued to our predetermined destination at Greenock but to everyone's dismay no leave was granted.

"The radio cables (aerials) of *Duchess* were later discovered to be wrapped around *Barham's* PVs."

Also on board *Barham* was Seaman Frank Loy: "There were terrible scenes as *Barham* lost way and rescue attempts were made. Sea boats were turned inboard, hampering lifesaving operations. Men screamed as they drowned in the cold waters, choked by spreading oil fuel. In these early days of the war no escape ports were provided in ships' sides and the capsized forward half of the destroyer presented stark horror as men screamed through the small scuttles as they passed astern to their deaths. *Barham* struck

45

Duchess between the forward funnel and the galley flat. Depth charges, not set to 'Safe' exploded in the after part of *Duchess* adding to the night's carnage. A young Midshipman and Leading Seaman Charlie Bishop both dived into the icy cold water to rescue several men; they were the heroes of the night. Other *Duchess* men survived by walking down their ship's side and stepping onto the side of *Barham* by the 6-inch starboard battery. It took until we reached Greenock to clean off the oil from the survivors whom we had plied with hot drinks liberally laced with rum."

Frank Henry Oliver was also on board the *Barham*: "*HMS Barham* escorted by four 'D' class destroyers was approaching the UK after eighteen months in the Mediterranean. During the morning watch (4am to 8am) at about 4.20am December 12th 1939 while proceeding through the Irish Sea the Squadron commenced the Zig Zag, a series of worked out compass courses to confuse enemy U-Boat captains, the *Barham* and three destroyers altered course on the executive signal correctly, but the *Duchess* went the opposite way, and before any avoiding action could be taken the *Barham's* bow crunched into her frail side. The impact seemed to me to be on the destroyer's starboard side, just for'ard of the bridge, she must have been terribly damaged. I rushed on deck and shouted to some seaman to get heaving lines and a chain jumping ladder. The *Duchess* was slithering along our port side and some of her ship's company who were on duty jumped from her decks to ours; we could hear and see other doomed men's white faces at the port-holes screaming in terror for help, but could do nothing to assist. It was an appalling sight as she dropped astern lost in the darkness and sinking rapidly. We heard cries for help so quickly threw the jumping ladder over the side, securing the inboard end, meanwhile some seaman had seen a couple of men in the sea and threw heaving lines to them, which they mercifully grabbed and were pulled towards the ladder and assisted inboard to safety. Next there were explosion astern which may have come from the doomed *Duchess* or other destroyers' depth charges in case U-boats were around. The survivors numbering about one officer and twenty men were taken to the sick-bay and made comfortable, approximately 120 officers and men had lost their lives, they having coming from the China Station with many gifts for their loved ones, but life, the most precious gift of all lost in this terrible disaster.

"More ships arrived and they thoroughly searched the area of the catastrophe while we proceeded to the River Clyde, a very saddened ship's company. Only *Barham* had the survivors, no other ships picked up anybody still alive.

"Later that day we anchored off Greenock, survivors were landed, and the *Barham* commenced normal routines of a warship on entering harbour: oiling etc. For myself, while in the Mediterranean, I had contracted some skin disease which would not heal. I saw the Medical Officer and he sent me to Kingseat Hospital, Aberdeen, where I arrived about the 14th December 1939."

*

Barham and her remaining four destroyers continued to Greenock where they waited at Toward Point for the all-clear to proceed through the mine-swept channel. Slowly the fleet made their way past the boom defence and took their own stations to anchor, securing to their respective replenishment ships to top up on fuel and essentials. Each ship set their torpedoes and depth charges to "safe" mode and continued their normal daily harbour routines.

Barham had anchored at around 12 noon and within an hour an oiler had secured alongside. With the events of the night fresh in everybody's mind, at 1400 a Court of Inquiry was convened on board.

Within twenty-four hours *Barham* was back at sea after reports of a large German force at sea caused the Commander In Chief (CinC) to sail his fleet comprising *Warspite*, *Hood* and *Barham* along with six destroyers and head back out. Two of those destroyers were *Duncan* and *Echo* who sailed the following day at 0855. *Duncan* log gives no mention of going alongside Greenock but 13 Dec log states they slipped from their oiler and headed back out to sea.

The Admiralty War Diary at the time gave the time of the collision at 0437 with the sinking at 0503 and made the following entries:

"*Barham* – Am proceeding with *Exmouth* and *Duncan*. *Eclipse* and *Echo* standing by till daylight have 24(?) survivors on board, *Exmouth* and *Duncan* have none. *Barham* struck *Duchess* a glancing blow abreast B Gun, eventually capsizing her but apparently not holing her to any marked extent."

*

One account of the loss of the *Duchess* was given by Ernest Swinhoe (in the official list of survivors this is spelled Swinhow) who was serving on board the *Barham*. The following was written by his daughter Wendy Middlemas and titled **The Death of a Duchess**...

It was an icy, black, December night and the destroyer, *Duchess* was heading home to the north of Scotland. Only another hour and she could dock at Greenock, at the end of a spectacular, record-breaking passage from East to West.

The declaration of war on Germany in that September of 1939 had been the signal for the flotilla of nine ships – all 'D' Class destroyers – to leave their Chinese port, with the instruction to set sail for the "friendly" waters of the U.K. with "the greatest possible speed."

It had been a rare experience, an impressive and morale-boosting sight for the crew of the *Duchess*, as they had steamed away in single file and at thirty knots, heading for refuelling at Singapore. On they had gone at break-neck speeds, beyond Colombo, Aden and into the Suez Canal.

Here, the other shipping had been halted to ensure the flotilla's unimpeded progress to Malta. At Malta, three of the destroyers – *Duchess*, *Dainty* and *Delight* – were detailed to escort the battleship *Barham* from Gibraltar to Scotland.

The *Barham* was a mighty ship. A veteran of previous skirmishes with the German fleet at Jutland in 1916. A massive vessel of some 31,000 tons, she dwarfed her escorting destroyers. The battleship and her escorts followed the usual pattern of submarine-avoidance by zigzagging, making it difficult for an enemy submarine to obtain a "fix" on the ship.

It had been a lightning trip - perhaps the fastest East-West passage ever recorded and the crew of the *Duchess* were rightly proud of their achievement, as, in the early gloom of a December morning, she zigged and zagged her way towards the Mull of Galloway.

The majority of the crew were below, asleep and the Petty Officer on watch had closed down all but one of the gunnery implacements, held a roll-call of his ten-gun crew and ordered them to go below, to secure their hammocks, to clear the way for their messmates at breakfast.

Only a young Ordinary Seaman, a "boy sailor" called Ernest Swinhoe, was left up top at the 'A' gun. He was the "communication number", the sailor on watch at the fore-gun. As the junior rating, he had been given the icy, early morning duty and he envied his gunnery mates their chance to go below into the warmth of the mess.

Ern had been lucky to join this destroyer, to be a part of the friendly crew of the *Duchess*, along with his good friend Peter Port. Peter was his best mate, the lad who had shown him the sights of Hong Kong, before they had left the East,

They had both felt privileged to be a part of this record-breaking destroyer flotilla. As an electrician, Peter was fortunate, he thought, to be below in the warmth of the low power room. Safe from the biting chill of a Scottish strait.

It was 0400 hours now, and the watch had begun. Only an hour of this and they would be home and dry. Ern stood in the shelter of the gun shield, to avoid the wind.

There was a blackout and the absence of moonlight made it a coal-black night. He adjusted his headphones and looked aft. It was then that he saw the massive shape of a ship's prow bearing down on him out of the darkness.

It towered over the diminutive destroyer and, with a sickening sound, hit the *Duchess* at about half way and with such tremendous speed that she simply turned the destroyer over. As she "turned turtle" Ern dived into the cold black sea, as other, half-naked sailors scrambled desperately round the rolling hull.

The *Barham's* searchlight lit up the scene. It had been her towering form that had pushed the *Duchess* over. Her crew felt sure that they had hit an enemy submarine, as the *Duchess's* upturned asdic dome looked just like a conning tower.

But, when her searchlight beam moved aft, it revealed the awful truth – the sight of a ship's screws, still turning – and her horrified crew began to sweep for survivors. The water was freezing and oil-ridden. There had been no time to grab lifebelts and Ern pushed off his rubber boots and overcoat, alternately treading water and floating on his back.

Out of the blackness, a drowning shipmate struggled towards him. He was naked and desperate and Ern realized from his "Ganges" training that the condemned boy would use him as a lifebelt – and so, condemn them both.

Ern swam away to a reasonable distance, until the poor fellow disappeared. The light from the *Barham* lit up the side of the upturned *Duchess* and Ern could clearly see the faces of frightened men, shouting through tiny portholes, from which they were unable to escape. On the fast-disappearing hull of the *Duchess* men were clinging on, until the *Barham* pulled alongside, plucking them to safety, only moments before the boilers of the *Duchess* blew and she disappeared beneath the waves, taking her entombed crew with her.

The *Barham* and her other destroyer escorts lowered boats and Ern began to shout to them. He realized that he had been in the water for some time now. His chances of survival were diminishing for every minute he was left in that icy waste. Suddenly, he heard the sound of a rowing boat and a coxswain shouting, "Oars!"

The men stopped rowing now and the coxswain shouted again for silence. Ern summoned up what little strength he had left and called for help. He was aware of a ship's lifeboat coming alongside and pairs of arms reaching out to pull him into the craft. He felt numb as the cold air hit him and he pleaded with his rescuers to put him back into the water, where it had felt warmer. When he reached the safety of the *Barham* he was a shaking mass, unable to warm himself through.

He was severely hypothermic and had been lucky to survive. His rescuers had pulled him out of the water at some minutes after 0500 hours, which meant that he had been in the water for an hour – beyond a reasonable amount of survival time for conditions such as those on that December night.

As he recovered, Ern learned that he was one of only twenty-three survivors from the ill-fated *Duchess* and her crew of a hundred and sixty men. His fate had rested on the timing of his watch duty.

He had possibly been the only sailor aboard to see the fateful collision, when the zig and zag of the two vessels had coincided. His heart went out to his mate, Peter Port, who had been below at the point of impact. He couldn't possibly have survived and Ern hoped that he had known little of what was happening as he and a hundred and twenty-three others perished in what was officially described at the time as, "One of those unfortunate accidents of war." More than fifty years have passed since that accident and my father, Ordinary Seaman Ernest Swinhoe still remembers the events of December 12th 1939 as if it happened yesterday. He can recall the cold, misery and confusion.

The anguish of seeing entombed sailors shouting from tiny portholes, the pain of losing a good friend and the guilt of seeing a shipmate drown before his eyes.

Since that day, however, ships have had escape hatches built into their sides, to prevent the fate that befell many of the *Duchess* crew. While her demise had not been as "newsworthy" as that of the *Hood*, the *Bismarck*, or – later – the poor old *Barham* herself, lessons had been learnt from this awful night in 1939.

4. Aftermath

The sinking of the *Duchess* was not the first nor would it be the last warship to be sunk in 1939. She was the third destroyer to sink since the outbreak of war just over three months previously, the other two being *Blanche* and *Gypsy,* who were both victims of mines within weeks of each other. Worse still, the aircraft carrier *Courageous* and battleship *Royal Oak* were both sunk by U-boat attacks in the September and October with heavy loss of life. To lose this many ships in such a short space of time was not a good start to the war, but little did the British know that this would only get worse as the war dragged on and the names of warships that had become a household name, such as the battlecruiser *Hood* and aircraft carrier *Ark Royal,* would also fall victim to enemy action. On top of this the war had already claimed countless merchant vessels and even within eight hours of war being declared a U-boat had torpedoed and sunk the liner *Athenia,* killing 118 passengers and crew, many of them women and children fleeing back to the United States, the ship sailing before war was even declared.

But while the families of those lost on the *Duchess* were reeling from the news that their men were no longer coming home, the Royal Navy was already distracted with an even bigger issue that had been building up in the South Atlantic. For months an unknown German warship had been causing havoc for merchant vessels without being seen. With a captain who actually had good morals, he would warn the ships of his impending intentions to sink them and so allow the crews to escape before opening fire on their ships. Operating between the Atlantic and Indian Oceans this ship was leaving the top brass at the Admiralty scratching their heads until late into the night. Ships were sent to chase this mysterious raider and in December 1939 the net was closing in.

The day after the *Duchess* had gone down, the German pocket battleship *Admiral Graf Spee* was finally intercepted by the heavy cruiser *HMS Exeter* and the light cruisers *HMS Ajax* and *HMNZS Achilles* after an incredible search following the eventual total loss of nine merchant ships at the hands of the Germans. The battle which followed would hit front pages around the world, more so in the Uruguayan capital of Montevideo when the *Graf Spee* was forced to enter port for urgent repairs. Due to the country being neutral the ship was allowed just a few days in port before she had to leave, which was clearly not long enough for repairs to be carried out on the battle damage of a ship that size. In the meantime, word was out that an entire task force was waiting for her, ready to pounce the moment she was out of Uruguayan territorial waters. With very few options left the captain sailed the ship out of harbour and came to a stop within sight of land, taking off her crew. With crowds lining the shore expecting a huge battle, they were granted an even more spectacular sight as suddenly explosions rocked the ship and lit up the evening sky as scuttling charges laid by the crew were detonated, sinking the ship and providing images of the burning vessel a guaranteed newspaper front page victory and a great reason to celebrate for the British.

As for the huge task group waiting for her…it was never there. The entire story was fabricated to make the Germans think there was no way out and the result was better than expected. The entire episode was later made into a film *The Battle of the River Plate* starring Anthony Quayle and Peter Finch.

With the drama of the *Graf Spee* chase making front pages for the next few days it was inevitable that the accidental loss of a destroyer in the Irish Sea would be pushed to the side to make room for a more morale-boosting victory. On Thursday 14th December the Admiralty announced the loss of the *Duchess* and the press reports first published the lists of those lost and saved. Buried within the other war reports, the details of her loss were barely even touched upon.

Behind closed doors the sudden loss of a warship that hadn't even been in the UK for the last five years was turning into a nightmare, when trying to locate people who may or may not have been on board. The fort in Malta known as *HMS St Angelo* was directing information on casualties to the Admiralty and requesting clarification of names and the correct forms to be filled out, in order to issue death certificates with the date of death being given as 12th December. This task became easier said than done.

The first job they had was to locate two ratings who may or may not have been on board. Stoker WG Kirk had been drafted to the *Duchess* on 22nd November 1938; another one they needed details on was JW Howes. They contacted two other ships, the heavy cruiser *Kent* and gunboat *Tarantula* as it was believed they were now serving on them. Thankfully both ratings were success-fully located and confirmed as not having been on board; Howes was found to be serving on the *Tarantula* but this was not known for sure until 17th December – five whole days after the sinking of *Duchess*.

Locating the Chinese crew became a matter of finding out who was on board, it later being realised that none of the five stewards and two canteen staff had survived. (The two canteen staff Cheung Chakman and Cheling Shing were never on the official list of those who died; it was while searching through the National Archives in 2018 that the names appeared, with two different names being originally Chung Chak and Ah Lew before it was confirmed otherwise.) It was also reported that two mess boys and one Makeelearn (a young trainee) were also on board but their names were unknown. It has never been confirmed if these three people were accounted for or if they were already named.

The father of twenty-year-old able seaman Hector Young was still writing letters on Christmas Day to the navy to try and find out the whereabouts of his son. The official explanation was that he was heading to the UK on board the troop ship *Franconia* but nobody had heard a thing from him. After an investigation taking several weeks he was later found to have actually been on the *Duchess* at the time of the collision and had not been one of the survivors. The confusion was brought about after the ship had on board two ratings with the name Young: HJ Young and JE Young. It was almost mid January 1940 when the confirmation came that there had been a mistake and that Hector Young had died on *Duchess*. The original signals from St Angelo made no mention of JE Young after the disaster. The navy contacted Hector's family and expressed deep regret for the mistake and the delay in informing the family of the loss of their son, which had caused them an incredible amount of anxiety and stress. He was not officially added to the list of casualties until 27th January 1940.

*

The death toll of the sinking of *HMS Duchess* was now 136, with just twenty-three survivors. Lt Pritchard RNVR was the only officer to survive; he was the one who had joined in Malta less than two months previously. Twelve ratings were now known to have been taken off the ship for various reasons in the weeks leading up to the sinking. Some were taken off for medical reasons and sent to hospitals in Malta and Gibraltar, others were lent to other ships to cover shortfalls in manpower. Little did they know as they were taken to hospital that they would be the extremely lucky ones.

Those lost in the *Duchess* would be remembered in different ways by their families. One such crew member was Leading Telegraphist Albert Henry Mann. He had been a member of the Gun Carriage Crew for the funeral of King George V on 28th January 1936 and had received the Royal Victorian Medal for his services on that occasion.

The family of George Taylor had various members of the family join the navy long after he had died. His photograph sat on the sideboard of his young nephew Geoffrey Mounstephen throughout his early life. He would often see his other uncle, Edward come home on leave and was inspired to join the navy himself as an artificer apprentice in 1955 at the age of sixteen, and ended up doing a career of thirty-eight years, eventually retiring as a Commander with an OBE.

Ordinary Seaman Kenneth Hoult became the first serviceman from Tamworth to lose his life in the war and was also one of the youngest. His parents received a message of sympathy from the King and Queen, details of their loss being published in the Tamworth Herald on 23rd December. Today his name can be found on both the Chatham Naval Memorial and in his home town on the Second World War plaque in St Editha's Parish Church.

Another Tamworth resident at the time of the loss was Sergeant Sydney Millerchip of the Royal Marines. He was serving on board the *Barham* on the night of the disaster and will have not only been shocked by the collision but most likely will have known that a fellow townsman will have been one of those lost.

Of the twenty-three survivors, two of these would be lost at sea during the war: William Robertson died in May 1942 when the submarine *HMS Olympus* was sunk off Greece and Donald Walter Cogger rose to the rank of Chief Petty Officer before being killed on board *HMS Wryneck* on 27th April 1941, aged forty. The only other details known are that he was the son of Walter and Eliza Cogger, husband of Dorothy Cogger of Gravesend, Kent.

Sophia Tilden, the wife of Engineering Officer Lt Tilden was later remarried after the war to a George R. Hunter.

The captain of the *Duchess* died leaving a grand total of £23,342 10s 7d to his seventy-five-year-old father, the baronet Sir Robert Eaton White who had previously been chairman of the Suffolk County Council. He would die the following year on 5th August 1940 and the family's beloved home at Boulge Hall soon became derelict. Surplus to requirements and heading into disrepair, the building was demolished in 1955.

*

Of the nine destroyers of the D class only the *Duncan* and *Decoy* were to survive the war. *Daring* was sunk on 18th February 1940 by a U-boat with the loss of 157 of her 162 crew. Just a few months later the *Delight* was hit in an air attack off Portland and went down on 29th July.

Decoy and Diana were both transferred to the Royal Canadian Navy in 1940, being renamed Kootenay and Margaree respectively. Kootenay was scrapped in 1946 but Margaree was involved in a collision with a merchant ship in the North Atlantic, sinking with the loss of 140 of her crew of 171.

During the evacuation from Greece the Diamond was sunk with heavy loss of life in an air attack on 27th April 1941

Off the coast of North Africa, 1941 saw two sisters go down due to the countless enemy air attacks, Dainty sinking on 24th February and Defender on 11th July, the latter having to be scuttled due to the amount of damage sustained in the raid; incredibly both ships did not sustain a high death toll, unlike their sister ships. Dainty's death toll was sixteen and in Defender none of her crew had been killed.

The lucky one was the Duncan, she had survived several collisions including two in the China Station before the war and suffered damage during a crash with a merchant ship during convoy duty in January 1940 but was towed back to Invergordon, Scotland, where she was repaired and sent back out to sea. After an eventful career she was eventually sold for scrap in 1945.

For the ship that had rammed and sunk the Duchess the war would be considerably different for a ship of her size. As a battleship it was inevitable that the Barham would be called upon to take part in major campaigns in which she sustained damage in several incidents including a torpedo hit. By the following year she was back sailing away from UK waters to spend the rest of the war in the Mediterranean. She would never return.

On 25th November 1941 during convoy hunting operations in a central Mediterranean task group she was hit by torpedoes from the German submarine U-331. She rolled over and exploded with over 850 of her crew dead – there were 487 survivors. The entire drama was caught on camera by one of the escorting ships and provides a shocking record of the horrors of the war at sea.

*

H64 would not be the last ship to be named *Duchess*. The name was once again used for the fifth time when a Daring Class Fleet Destroyer was launched in 1951. She served the Royal Navy until 1964 when she was loaned to the Royal Australian Navy as a replacement for the destroyer *Voyager* which had been sunk in a collision, serving her new owners in the Far East until 1973 when she was converted for use as a training ship until she was finally decommissioned in 1977 and sold for scrap in 1980.

The wreck of the *Duchess* was located in 1966 during a survey and again it showed up on a sonar reading in 1973, but it was the Royal Navy survey ship *HMS Bulldog* which identified her on 7th June 1984 using side scan sonar which allowed the teams to measure the wreck and positively identify her as the lost *Duchess*. Intact and almost upright, she is lying at a general depth of 119m with a height from the seabed of 8.2m with no scour. Her position is 55 21.865N, 06 02.71W pointing at 110 degrees. At the time of writing there are no visual images of the wreck, we can only hope that one day cameras will be sent down to bring back images of her silent guns and damaged hull. In 1989 for the 50th anniversary of the sinking several relatives of those who died on board the ship were taken out to the wreck site on board the patrol vessel *HMS Ranger*. On board were relatives of George Wilkie, Stephen Walsh and Gordon Godfrey. Together a short service of remembrance was conducted by the Reverend Desmond Hanna and the relatives of those lost cast their memorial wreaths into the sea.

For the crew of the *Duchess* there is a memorial window commemorating the loss of the ship and her crew at the Church of Saint Michael in Boulge, Suffolk. The words at the bottom say:

Sacred to the memory of Lieut Comdr Robert Charles Meadows White, Royal Navy. Eldest son of Sir Robert White Lt and Lady White of Boulge Hall and of the officers and ships' Company of HMS Duchess which was sunk in active service December 12 1939.

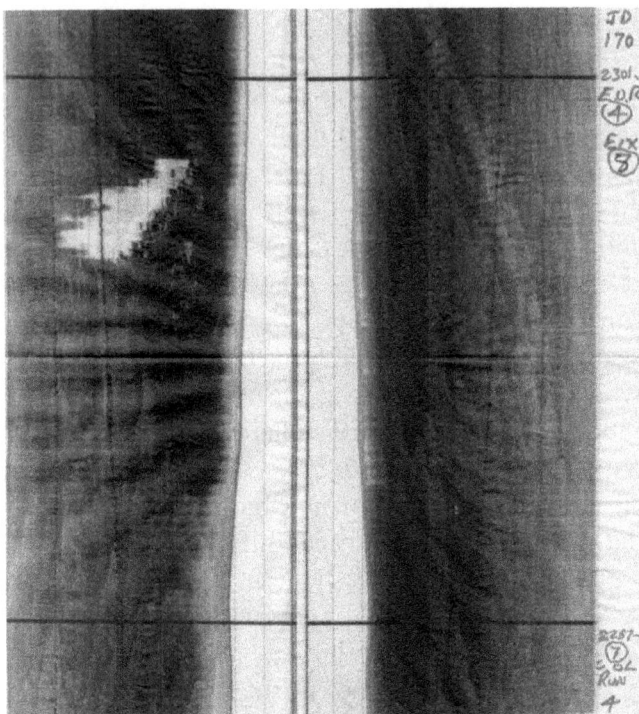

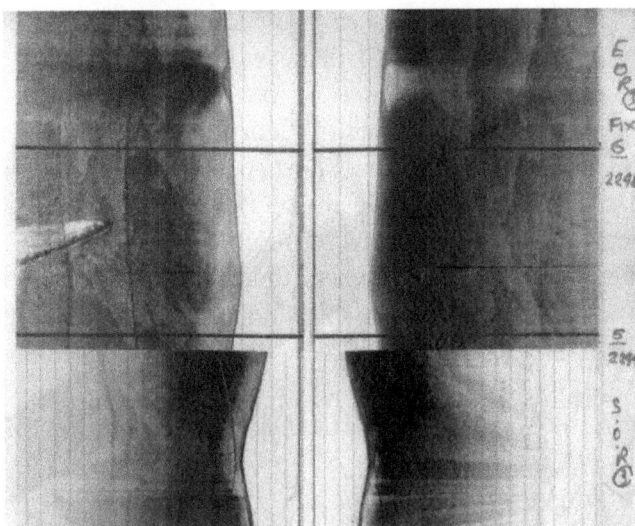

Sonar images show the wreck of *Duchess* on the seabed during a routine survey.

60

1939

HMS   BLANCHE
HMS   DUCHESS
HMS   GIPSY

Chatham Memorial

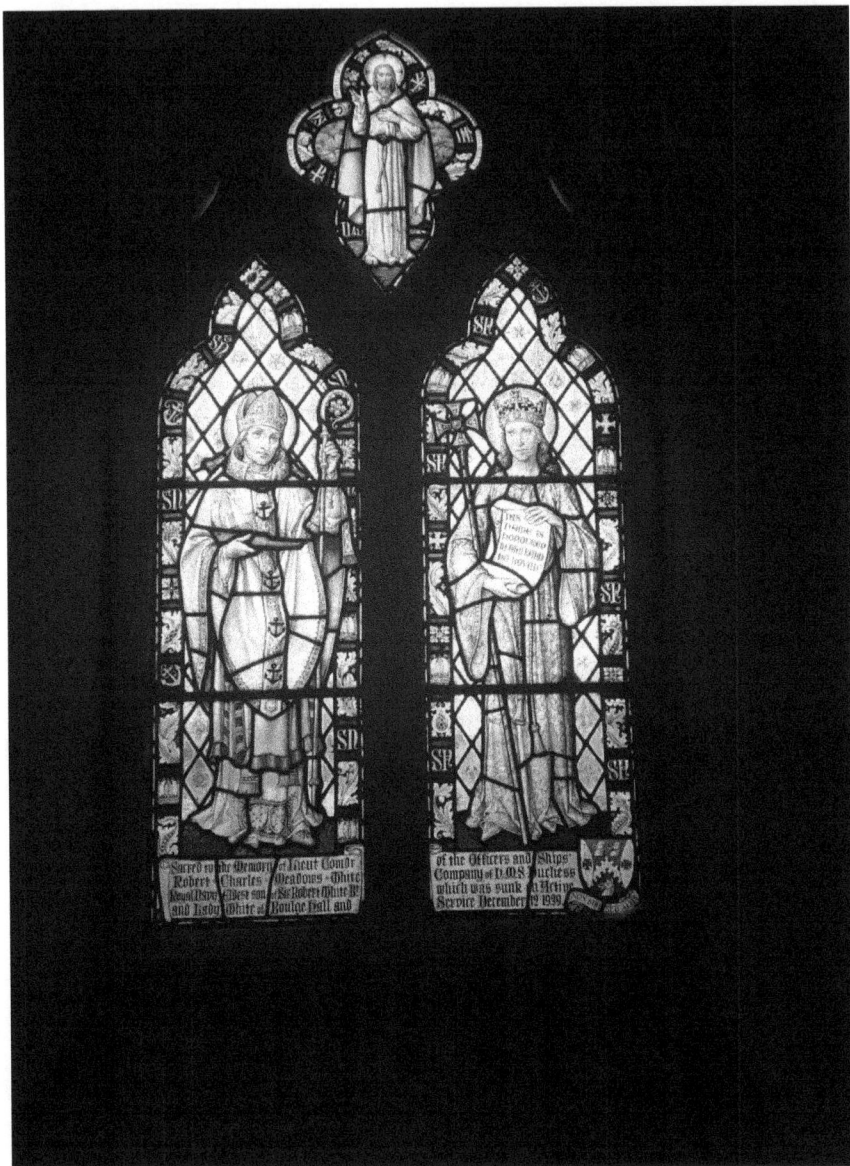

Memorial window at the Church of Saint Michael in Boulge, Suffolk.

The name *HMS Duchess* was later used for another destroyer - here she is in 1969
after being lent to the Royal Australian Navy to replace a ship lost in a collision.

Acknowledgements

Ray Hoult
Colin Motton
Peggy Harper
Peter Sabean
Victor Fox
Geoffrey John Mounstephen OBE
Tito Vallejo
Gordon Smith
Guildhall Library
Royal Naval Association
National Museum of the Royal Navy
Maritime Picture Library
Luis Photos (Gibraltar)
Church of Saint Michael, Boulge, Suffolk
UK Hydrographics Office
The National Archives.

National Archives sources

ADM 1/10135 – HMS Duchess report of proceedings Sharp Point 1938
ADM 53/108458 – Log of HMS Eclipse December 1939
ADM 53/108452 – Log of HMS Echo December 1939
ADM 53/108396 – Log of HMS Duncan December 1939
ADM 53/107659 – Log of HMS Barham December 1939
ADM 53/108384 – Logs of HMS Duchess September and October 1939
ADM 196/149483 – Robert Charles Meadows White (record of naval career)
ADM 358/3232 – Casualties HMS Duchess

Appendix

Convoy Blue 003

Blue 003 convoy – 30 Sept – 5 Oct 1939

Port Said 30 Sept 1939
Gibraltar 11 Oct 1939

Escort	From	To
Defender	30 September	5 October
Duchess	30 September	5 October
Fowey	30 September	11 October
Grenade	5 October	8 October
Griffin	5 October	8 October
Grimsby	30 September	11 October

List of those killed on HMS Duchess 12 December 1939

Surname	Forename	Age	Rank
ABBOTT	THOMAS ALFRED	39	Stoker 1st Class
AH FONG			Leading Steward
AH TAT			Steward
ALLEN	JOHN CHARLES	20	Telegraphist
ANDERSON	ROBERT HORNBY	19	Ordinary Seaman
ANDREWS	HERBERT WILLIAM	30	Leading Cook (S)
BACON	HERBERT JAMES	19	Able Seaman
BAINES	ARTHUR LEONARD		Leading Seaman
BANGAY	ERIC		Able Seaman
BANNING	FREDERICK JOHN		Stoker 1st Class
BARBER	ROBERT WILLIAM	39	Petty Officer
BARNES	DAVIDSON BELL		Able Seaman
BARSTARD	PERCY RICHARD	19	Ordinary Seaman
BASHFORD	FRANK	36	Chief Stoker
BATEMAN	THOMAS JOHN BENJAMIN		Able Seaman
BIGGIN	CYRIL CHARLES	31	Leading Seaman
BLOUNT	WILLIAM THOMAS JOHN	18	Ordinary Seaman
BOND	RICHARD		Able Seaman
BRASS	ROBERT BEDFORD	28	Engine Room Artificer 3rd Class
BRIDGER	CYRIL JOHN	24	Leading Stoker
BROADWAY	ALBERT		Able Seaman
BROCKMAN	ERNEST STEPHEN		Stoker 1st Class
BROMHEAD	ERNEST HENRY JACK		Signalman
BROWN	GEORGE		Able Seaman
BURGESS	ALBERT GRAHAM	22	Leading Seaman
BURT	WILLIAM HENRY	26	Leading Signalman
BURTON	THOMAS LESLIE		Able Seaman
CHALLIS	LEWIS FELDMAN	29	Petty Officer
CHAKMAN	CHEUNG		Canteen Manager
CHAPMAN	ALBERT EDWARD		Electrical Artificer 1st Class
CHEDZEY	BERNARD HUBERT	23	Leading Sick Berth Attendant
CHOI WEY			Petty Officer Steward
CLARK	DENIS PEVERILL		Leading Stoker
CLARK	WILLIAM CHARLES BOOTH	22	Able Seaman

66

CLEAVELY	JOHN GEORGE ALBERT		Able Seaman
CROOK	REGINALD VINCENT	35	Able Seaman
CROUCHER	EDWARD GEORGE		Able Seaman
DAWES	ALEC RAYDYN ARTHUR	29	Petty Officer
DE BOCK	STEPHEN JAMES	19	Ordinary Seaman
DIXON	VERNON JAMES		Petty Officer Cook (S)
DOCWRA	JOHN FREDERICK		Leading Seaman
DONALDSON	AUSTIN CLYDE		Petty Officer
DONOVAN	PATRICK WILLIAM FREDERICK GEORGE	19	Stoker 1st Class
DOWNS	EDWARD		Able Seaman
EATON	GEOFFREY	23	Able Seaman
EDDLESTON	HERBERT GRIFFITH		Ordinary Seaman
EMMINS	WILLIAM EDWARD	25	Able Seaman
FLACK	CHARLES EDWARD	20	Able Seaman
FORREST	GEORGE ALFRED		Ordinary Seaman
FORSDYKE	DOUGLAS RONALD		Leading Seaman
FOSTER	LESLIE	18	Ordinary Seaman
GILHAM	THOMAS	20	Stoker 1st Class
GINNS	HENRY ARTHUR	39	Leading Seaman
GLADING	PHILIP GORDON	24	Able Seaman
GODFREY	GORDON CLIFTON	33	Ordnance Artificer 1st Class
GORDON	HUGH PRICE	37	Gunner
GULSON	FRANK VERDUN	22	Able Seaman
HAIGH	DAVID WALTER		Stoker 1st Class
HALSTEAD	JOHN ROBERT	34	Petty Officer Stoker
HAMER	JAMES ARTHUR		Able Seaman
HARRISON	HERBERT ALEXANDER		Stoker 1st Class
HARRISON	JOHN		Stoker 1st Class
HARVEY	GEOFFREY RALPH DOUGLAS	20	Able Seaman
HAYWARD	PERCY SMAIL	25	Leading Stoker
HEBDON	LIONEL GEORGE THOMAS	20	Leading Seaman
HOPPER	REGINALD	29	Able Seaman
HOULT	KENNETH ARTHUR		Ordinary Seaman
INGALL	GEORGE HENRY	22	Able Seaman
JOHNSON	ROBERT		Able Seaman
JONES	WILLIAM THOMAS		Able Seaman
JOYCE	HERBERT	25	Telegraphist

KENLEY	GEORGE	21	Able Seaman
KINNINMONT	ROBERT RITCHIE		Engine Room Artificer 4th Class
KRETSCHMER	CEDRIC LEMBOURNE	19	Midshipman
LECKEY	JOSEPH	19	Able Seaman
LYNE	CHARLES HERBERT		Signalman
MACDERMOTT	RONALD ALBERT	22	Able Seaman
MANN	ALBERT HENRY		Leading Telegraphist
MILLS	SIDNEY NORMAN	29	Leading Seaman
MOORE	GEORGE	25	Stoker 1st Class
MORECRAFT	ALBERT FREDERICK	33	Able Seaman
MOUNTER	JOHN WILLIAM ISAAC	29	Petty Officer
MUNT	GEORGE THOMAS		Ordinary Seaman
MURRAY	GEORGE WINGATE	26	Lieutenant
MURTON	STANLEY JOHN CHARLES	21	Able Seaman
McMEEKIN	HAROLD		Ordinary Seaman
McNAMARA	EDWARD COWNDON	28	Leading Seaman
OATES	WILFRED LEONARD	20	Stoker 1st Class
PALMER	ALEXANDER CHARLES		Stoker 1st Class
PALMER	ERNEST CECIL	20	Able Seaman
PETERS	RALPH WILLIAM	19	Ordinary Seaman
PHILLIPS	MAURICE KEY		Leading Stoker
PORT	PETER WILLIAM	19	Able Seaman
PRATT	BERNARD ISAAC		Able Seaman
PRICE	KENNETH JOHN	18	Ordinary Seaman
PUPLETT	JAMES WILLIAM		Stoker 1st Class
RALPH	ROWALD WILLIAM THOMAS		Ordinary Seaman
READ	GEORGE EDWARD		Leading Seaman
REED	WILLIAM ARTHUR		Signalman
RIX	HARRY BENJAMIN COURTNEY	38	Chief Engine Room Artificer
ROBERTS	WILLIAM HAROLD		Able Seaman
ROBINSON	JOHN ROBERT BELL		Able Seaman
ROGERS	CLARENCE HENRY	39	Petty Officer Stoker
SAUNDERS	FRANK RUPERT		Able Seaman
SCHOLFIELD	JAMES MICHAEL LESLIE	22	Lieutenant
SCOTT	EDWARD WILLIAM GEORGE		Stoker 1st Class
SELBY	FREDERICK THOMAS	22	Stoker 1st Class

SHAUGH-NESSY	MICHAEL		Ordinary Seaman
SHIELDS	NEIL		Stoker 1st Class
SHING	CHELING		Canteen Assistant
SMITH	WILLIAM JAMES ARCHIBALD		Petty Officer Stoker
SPILLER	GEORGE SIDNEY ROBERT	26	Leading Supply Assistant
STEVENSON	JOHN DOUGLAS		Able Seaman
SULLIVAN	CORNELIUS	19	Stoker 2nd Class
SURRIDGE	REGINALD EDWARD	18	Ordinary Seaman
SUTTON	GEORGE ALBERT	26	Stoker 1st Class
TAYLOR	GEORGE EDWARD	21	Able Seaman
TAYLOR	VICTOR RONALD	23	Stoker 1st Class
THORNTON	WILLIAM	22	Able Seaman
TILDEN	OSMOND PETER	30	Lieutenant (E)
TURNBULL	WILLIAM	25	Able Seaman
WALKER	ERIC SHEARSTONE	37	Electrical Artificer 1st Class
WALSH	FLORENCE STEPHEN	24	Able Seaman
WARD	FRED DOUGLAS	38	Chief Petty Officer
WARD	THOMAS HAROLD	21	Able Seaman
WARNER	ALFRED SYDNEY	20	Able Seaman
WARR	EDWARD ARTHUR	19	Ordinary Seaman
WEBB	GEORGE	33	Petty Officer Stoker
WHITE	ROBERT CHARLES MEADOWS	34	Lieut-Commander
WILKIE	GEORGE	30	Leading Seaman
WILLIAMS	FREDERICK HENRY		Ordinary Seaman
WILLIAMS	SIDNEY		Petty Officer Supply
WILLIAMS	WILLIAM		Stoker 1st Class
WOOD	GEORGE EDMUND		Engine Room Artificer 3rd Class
WOOD	KENNETH		Engine Room Artificer 3rd Class
YOUNG	HECTOR JOHN	20	Able Seaman

Died at sea 15 September 1939

WALKER	WILLIAM	36	Stoker 1st Class

Duchess Survivors

Rank/Rate	Number	Name	Notes
AB	C/SSX 16954	Adams, Jack	
CPO	CJ 69276	Cogger, Donald W	Died 27 apr 1941 on sinking of *HMS Wryneck* in Battle of Greece
AB	C/JX 142768	Crowall, Charles	
Stoker 1st Class RFRB	18897	Crowther, George	
Ord. seaman	C/SSX 21525	Dodds, John E.	
LS	C/JX 134607	Durling, Alfred H	
AB	C/JX 14444B	Hale, Kenneth R.	
AB	C/JX 138679	Harris, Geoffrey	
AB	C/SSX 15479	Jenkins, Ivan	
AB	C/SSX 21227	Lawrence, Charles H	
AB RFRB	25414	Lowthorpe, John E	
LS	C/JX 127142	McHardy, Robert	
AB	C/JX 127588	Merry, Charles R	
LS	C/JX 131525	Moir, Harry	
Probationary Lt (RNVR)		Pritchard, JR	
Ord Seaman	C/SSX 27921	Proctor, Walter R	
AB	C/JX 142482	Ratcliffe, Trevor	
AB	C/SSX 19870	Robertson, William	Died May 1942 in sinking of submarine *HMS Olympus*
Telegraphist	C/JX 142461	Thurley, Clarence	
PO Stoker	C/K 50792	Tootel, Thomas	
AB	C/SSX 15981	Smith, Alfred	
Ord Seaman	C/JX 156254	Swinhow, Ernest	Service number reused 1942
CPO Stoker	C/K 58333	Willy, John A	

9 780244 112349